ADVENTURES
OF AN
AMATEUR
NATURALIST
IN MEXICO

The Imperial
Ivory-billed Woodpecker,
Revisited

Written by
GEORGE B. WINTON &
TODD BRUCE

Introduction by
TODD BRUCE

Black Swift Press
SANTA CRUZ, CALIF.

Black Swift Press
Santa Cruz, Calif.

Excerpt written by George B. Winton, licensed under Creative Commons

Original cover artwork by Sandy Tueller, acrylic on canvas

Still photographs of study skins courtesy A. F. Whitaker

Lithograph artwork of imperial woodpecker by Adele Henderson, adapted from the
Century Dictionary and Cyclopedia, 1898. Original artist unknown.

Design by Bri Bruce Productions
www.bribruceproductions.net

ADVENTURES
OF AN
AMATEUR
NATURALIST
IN MEXICO

The Imperial
Ivory-billed Woodpecker,
Revisited

In the spring of 2016, I was meticulously sifting through thousands of documents archived in the Smithsonian Institution while conducting research for *The Devil's Road: A Baja Adventure*, a documentary film I am producing. Working alongside the film's director, J.T. Bruce, we uncovered a gem of a document in an unmarked folder buried deep in the files of Dr. Edward William Nelson and Edward Alphonso Goldman, two of America's most prolific—though obscure—naturalists. To our knowledge it has not seen the light of day since its first writing and has never been published.

We felt the need to bring it out of hiding and include it herein in its entirety.

Our film, *The Devil's Road* retraces the landmark 1905 and 1906 expedition of Nelson and Goldman, who became two of the more important mammalogists in America in the early 20th Century—yet are little known outside of academic circles. They journeyed over 2,000 miles on horseback to collect specimens on behalf of the Smithsonian Institution, under the employ of the United States Biological Survey to study the flora and fauna of the Baja California Peninsula. This was, at the time, a region largely unknown to science and considered one of the most remote and unwelcoming sections of North America.

Nelson and Goldman were dispatched to Mexico in January of 1892 for what was to be a three-month excursion. The pair's assignment was to determine the feasibility of natural history exploration in that region of the world. The U.S. Biological Survey was attempting to better understand North America's flora and fauna and their corresponding geographical distribution with a keen interest in migratory birds and animals and the habitat range of plants. Nelson and Goldman's three-month visit transformed into a fourteen-year expedition through all of Mexico culminating in the Baja Peninsula. This would be the first time they could discuss, with much confidence, the relations and distribution of Mexico's plants and animals. The findings of these field surveys were foundational efforts of a conservation movement that helped solidify the work of the U.S. Biological Survey and conservationists like John Muir, Theodore Roosevelt, and Gifford Pinchot.

Within two days of Nelson and Goldman landing in Manzanillo, Mexico, they found and collected a specimen previously unknown to science: a large narrow-headed, tree-climbing rat in the forest skirting the town's port. *Hodomys alleni*, the Allen's woodrat, was the first endemic Mexican species they discovered in Mexico[1]. This initial success set the tone for their field studies there, thus providing the energy, drive, and support to continue to study the country's interior.

In an environment where unique plants and animals thrive, Mexico is as diverse as they come. The fifth most biologically diverse country in the world, out of only seventeen, Mexico is considered ecologically megadiverse. You can find Mexico, together with Brazil, Colombia, and Indonesia, on the very top of the list taking up the first place in reptile diversity, second in mammals, fourth in amphibians and vascular plants, and tenth in birds[2].

From grizzly bears to small rodents, many animals that once flourished, however, are now extinct—and many more are on the brink. The vaquita (*Phocoena sinus*), one of the planet's smallest cetaceans, is one such example. With its range confined to only the delta region of the Sea of Cortez, recent surveys indicate there is an estimated population of only 12 individuals remaining[3]. It may, too, soon be extinct.

There are other Mexican animals that have long been thought to be extinct, but until recently have been found alive, though struggling to survive with very low population numbers. The tiny Nelson's small-eared shrew (*Cryptotis nelsoni*) is one case. This 10-centimeter-long rodent was discovered on the slopes of the San Martin Tuxtla volcano in Veracruz, Mexico, by Nelson and Goldman in 1894. They collected twelve specimens of this never-before-seen shrew on its western slope at around 4,500 feet of elevation. These were the only animals ever collected until 2004 when a small population was rediscovered[4].

Together, Nelson and Goldman crossed and recrossed the length and breadth of Mexico on their expedition, eventually visiting every state and territory of the republic. Many of these areas had never been visited by scientists before. The pair completed the most extensive and focused scientific exploration of any single country and conducted the most complete collection of birds, animals, reptiles, and plants that has ever been gathered. Over 30,000 mammal and bird specimens and thousands of plant collections were made. Many plants and animals new to science were discovered, and Nelson named 72 Mexican mammal taxa, 53 of those in collaboration with Goldman. Goldman named an additional 117 Mexican taxa alone[5].

One particularly important stop on Nelson and Goldman's expedition was Patzcuaro, Michoacan, in October of

E. A. Goldman's handwritten field notes, mention of the imperial woodpecker (Campephilis imperialis) noted. Smithsonian Institution archives.

THE AUK:

A QUARTERLY JOURNAL OF

ORNITHOLOGY.

VOL. XV.   JULY, 1898.   NO. 3.

THE IMPERIAL IVORY-BILLED WOODPECKER,
CAMPEPHILUS IMPERIALIS (GOULD).

BY E. W. NELSON.

Plate III.

AT A meeting of the Zoölogical Society of London, held on August 14, 1832, specimens were exhibited of a previously undescribed Woodpecker, remarkable for its extraordinary size. These specimens, the male of which measured two feet in length, were said to have been obtained by Mr. Gould from "that little explored district of California which borders the territory of Mexico"—a statement which serves as a good illustration of the vague ideas of American geography that prevailed among naturalists in those days. Mr. Gould made a felicitous choice of name when he called this bird *Picus imperialis* for it is by far the largest and most striking member of the Woodpecker family in the world. The authors of the 'Biologia Centrali-Americana' say that Gould's original skins are made up like those of Floresi, a mining engineer, who collected birds in the Sierra Madre Mountains near Bolaños, Jalisco, early in the century. My own observations prove that the Imperial Ivory-bill is found near that place, and there is little doubt that it is the type locality. The home of this Woodpecker is in such a remote and rarely visited region that despite the large size and conspicuous plumage of the bird, many years passed after its discovery before any additions

E. W. Nelson's article in the July 1898 Volume 15 No. 3
issue of The Auk: A Quarterly Journal of Ornithology.

1892. Arriving at the train station to accompany the two naturalists were Mr. George Winton and his assistant, intent on joining them for a pleasure hunting trip. Four saddle horses and two mules were outfitted for a nearly three-week expedition into the Nahuatzen mountain range. It was on this collecting trip that the group came across, for the first time, several individuals of the world's largest woodpecker: the imperial woodpecker (*Campephilus imperialis*). No one in the party had ever seen one, but Nelson knew of the bird and recognized it immediately upon their first sighting.

In July of 1898, *The Auk: A Quarterly Journal of Ornithology* published a paper written by Nelson about the imperial woodpecker. Titled *The Imperial Ivory-Billed Woodpecker, Campephilus imperialis (Gould)* he describes the bird, it's habitat and habits, and his experiences during the collecting trip in 1892 with Winton. This document is an impressive, first-of-its-kind view into the life and habits of this bird and includes a beautiful painting by J. L. Ridgway of two imperials (a male and female) hitched on the side of a dead tree.

"The natural history of the imperial woodpecker practically begins and ends with Nelson and Goldman," writes Tim Gallagher in *Imperial Dreams: Tracking the Imperial Woodpecker Through the Wild Sierra Madre*. It was in Nelson and Goldman's archived files and documents where we came across this type script eight-page manuscript written by Winton. It was lightly edited with pencil and lying in a nondescript folder with no signifiers with only a handwritten note on the last page that was first written in ink then scratched out and finished in pencil. I have added herein those changes.

Winton's document excellently portrays the mindset of the "naturalist" in the late nineteenth century. Compared to today's methods and standards, the use of a shotgun as a collecting tool—and the belief that a species close to extinction is better killed and purposed as a preserved specimen for science than left to an uncertain future—may seem draconian.

We have no real understanding of George Winton; there is no indication as to how Nelson and Winton knew each other. The only evidence we found was a line in Goldman's field notes describing Winton as a man of the church and a journalist. This is Winton's account of their search for the imperial woodpecker.

by Geo. B. Winton
San Luis Potosi, Mexico
Circa, 1892

There are not many forests of large trees in Mexico. The tropical vegetation is usually a dense jungle overtopped by trees of low growth. It is a peculiar pleasure, therefore, for the traveler in this republic to get among the tall pines, fine groves of which

J.L. Ridgway

$\frac{1}{4}$

IMPERIAL WOODPECKER ♂ & ♀
(CAMPEPHILUS IMPERIALIS GOULD.)

A Hoen & Co. Lithocaustic. Baltimore

*Artist J. L. Ridgway's painting of an imperial woodpecker in
E. W. Nelson's article in the July 1898 Volume 15 No. 3
issue of* The Auk: A Quarterly Journal of Ornithology.

crown some of the higher mountain ranges.

The Sierra de Michoacan is a crescent shaped range of irregular volcanic hills, from eight to twelve thousand feet high, mostly covered with a rich deep soil, on which grow magnificent pine forests. These usually clothe the hills to the very top, only a few peaks protruding above timber line. This sierra lies almost entirely within the state from which it takes its name, one of the middle western states of the Republic, and the length of its crescent is about one hundred and fifty miles.

Mr. E. W. Nelson, a scientist whose work in Alaska gave him a national reputation, has been for some years in Mexico in the interest of the United States National Museum. A trip which I made with him to the forest region above described in the autumn of 1892 was my introduction to practical scientific work.

The train carried us to Patzcuaro, a town which, with the beautiful lake of the same name, lies far within the crescent curve of the mountain chain. It is the terminus of a branch of the Mexican National Railway. We climbed the long hill from the station to the town in the warm yellow light of the setting sun, stopping often to look back upon the lovely scene of lake and pine-clad mountains which spread out behind us. On the little round islands of the lake, as well as dotting its margin, lie a multitude of fisher villages. The red tiles of the roofs, the deep green foliage of the trees - aguacates, zapotes, chirimoyas, nueces, and others - and the whitewashed walls of the houses, all flashed in the still waters of the lake. These fisher people are pure Tarascan Indians, speaking the same language and living the same life as when Cortes landed at Vera Cruz. The same tribe is scattered all through the sierra, and is very numerous.

That night we chaffered with a fletero of picturesquely villainous aspect. Horses for ourselves and mules for our baggage were the subjects of earnest consideration. To beat down the exorbitant prices first asked to a reasonable figure, required hours of laborious offers and counter offers. Finally a bargain was struck, and we went to bed to sleep the sleep of men who have got rid of a great burden.

Next morning we set out, fringing the lake for several miles, and crossing an arm of it on a causeway. Then we began to climb out of the basin, leaving far below us the shining waters, that reflecting the brightness of the sky and contrasted with the dark hills, looked like molten silver. Up, up, over hills of white volcanic ash piles of rough stones, through cultivated fields on the mesas, higher and higher we rode, while the view behind us widened and brightened with the climbing sun. The trees grew thicker. First were Madronos, oaks, hawthorns, and the rough pinon; then the out-flanking skirmishers of the army of long-leaf pines, till at the top of the range as we crossed over to the western slope, we met the main body itself, waving long arms and singing solemnly in the sweet, cool air.

We rode down a slight incline through fields of wheat, to pass a village embowered in orchards of wild cherries, apples and pears. The fruit of the wild cherry (capulina) is better in Mexico than in the United States, and is highly valued. These cool hill country villages have a climate suited to growing apples, which in most of the country do not do well. But the people know nothing of the proper care of the trees. They leave them to grow unpruned and uncultivated, till the orchard becomes a perfect jungle. I was interested in the fact that the pears were all grafted in the stock of the hawthorn, a large species of which, bearing a yellow fruit, but otherwise similar to that of the Mississippi Valley, is common in this country. It looked odd to see large trees, bearing at the top little brown pears, while the boughs that came out near the ground bore yellow haws [sic], - tecocotes.

But the most curious and interesting thing to be seen in these mountain villages are the houses. My readers know, I am sure, that the typical Mexican house is a hut of adobe, or mud bricks, with a sod roof and a dirt floor. Imagine therefore my surprise and delight to find these Tarascan Indians

Houses of the Tarascan indians, as described in
Winton's account, taken circa 1892, likely by Goldman.
Lantern slide on glass.

living in neatly finished wood cottages, with sloping roofs of "shake," or spit shingles, held in place by wooden pegs, and smooth floors of large puncheons or hewn slabs, raised some distance above the ground. The walls are made of wide beams, carefully hewn with the adze, about four inches by a foot in size, and as long as it is desired to make the side of the house. These are carefully dovetailed at the corners of the building, and so well adjusted that the wall is practically air-tight. These neat cottages only lack glass windows and open fire-places to make them entirely cosy. As it is, they are far superior to any indigenous houses I have seen. Many of them have verandas in front with carved wooden pillars, between which hang pots of flowers. These simple people have an innate fondness for flowers, which shows itself in many ways.

From the village, Pichataro, we passed up a long slope into the big trees again. We had just stopped to drink at a fresh little mountain brook, and were riding along a mesa where many trees had been girdled and killed to make a clear-

ing, when a fine big bird flew across in front of us with the peculiar swoop of the woodpeckers, and swung himself up against the side of a dead pine in the clearing.

Nelson pulled his horse up suddenly and looked at me with round eyes. "Man!" he said, "we must have that fellow."

"What is it?" I replied, my own interest aroused.

"That is the Imperial Ivorybill Woodpecker (Campephilus imperialis), the biggest woodpecker in the world, and very rare. I suppose not a dozen altogether could be found in the museums of America and Europe."

He spoke with such confidence that I supposed he must be familiar with the bird. I was a good deal surprised to be told later that he had never seen one before. Such is the naturalist's eye. No wonder Agassiz kept a student looking for three days at one little fish.

We dismounted in great excitement. I was carrying my gun across the saddle, and Nelson insisted that I should take the responsibility of securing this treasure. Just then we noticed to our delight that the bird's mate was on the trunk with him. I slipped two cartridges loaded with number 6 shot, and crept near. The bird paid but little attention to me. The fine red crest of the male caught my eye, and I aimed at him carefully, flattering myself that I should catch the female as she started to fly. At the roar of the gun the bark and dust flew off in a cloud, and to my astonishment out of it swept my quarry with a chipper cry, as if to be sprinkled with an ounce of shot was an everyday affair with him. As soon as I could catch my breath, I let drive at him the other barrel. One of the little pellets of shot broke his wing, and he swung down with angry yells to the ground, where Nelson and I both pounced on him. He whisked over on his back, opened his great yellow bill and squalled viciously. His eyes glittered and his blood-red crest waved fiercely. It was only after we had scuffled with and choked him for several minutes that he succumbed. Meantime his partner had taken herself off, though not till she had lingered and scolded for some time.

That night our prize was carefully skinned and prepared for preservation. I watched the operation with deep interest, for it was new to me. The skill which can be attained by practice at this difficult art is as surprising as the keenness and readiness of vision acquired by the trained naturalist.

Mr. Nelson made his camp on a high ridge just west of the village of Nahuatzen. I was detained in the village for two days, after which I joined him. There were plenty of the birds, - pitoreales, the natives call them, as we were assured, so he waited for me to secure some additional specimens. I entered upon this commission with great readiness. It gratified my taste for hunting, which is strong enough even when there is no special object in view.

The forests were delightful. The great tree trunks, many of them from four to six feet in diameter, towered high into the air, which was cool and clear. Across the cultivated valleys lying far beneath, we could see the other pine-clad hills rising one behind the other into the blue distance. Villages nestled

Top: Study skin of an imperial woodpecker (C. imperialis)*, second from right, beside ivorybill woodpecker* (C. principalis)*. Bottom: Tags of study skins,* C. imperialis *in background. Photos by A. F. Whitaker. University of Kansas Museum of Natural History.*

Hand-printed lithograph of imperial woodpecker (C. imperialis) with additions by Adele Henderson. Adapted from the Century Dictionary and Cyclopedia, 1898.

here and there at the foot of the mountains, dark with the foliage of fruit trees, and veiled in the thin wisps of smoke. Around them spread the brown and yellow and green squares of the fields, some of them lying fallow but most of them in maize, just beginning to ripen. These villagers and farmer people, holding their lands in severalty and cultivating them themselves, and are in consequence of a more independent and hardy character than the poor peons on large haciendas, or even the laborers in the cities.

To these glorious views of which we never tired, were added the comforts of an ideal camp. We had great blazing log fires, and our tent was pitched on a carpet of pine straw.

The birds I set out to look for are fond of open spaces, and the dead trees that still stand in them. These hills belong to the various villages in community, each village commune holding at least one wooded mountain for a stock range, wood supply, etc. The natives are like people the world over in that they have no realization of the value and glory of a forest - at least not till it is gone. So they cut down and girdle and hack and burn these grand trees till it makes ones heart ache. To clear a little place for a corn or barley patch, which perhaps is soon abandoned to the gophers, they destroy thousands of dollars worth of lumber, and make an end of trees that have been hundreds of years in growing.

I wandered about through these openings, finding the objects of my search with no great difficulty. But I was rather chagrined at banging at several fine fellows without getting them. I did not know whether to blame myself, the gun, or the cartridges. The gun had been well tried and was from one of the best American factories. The cartridges contained the load I usually employ in duck shooting. As for myself, I thought it likely I might sometimes have miscalculated distances, for the trees were amazingly tall. But after making all qualification I concluded that this particular bird is very tough and hard to kill.

I came one afternoon upon a pair of ivorybills in a little hill-side field. The male flew away with a loud chatter. I fired at the female, and she came to the ground with a broken wing. I immediately dashed upon her, not wishing to mar the feathers with another shot. She got into the fence, which was made of huge logs piled lengthwise and covered with brush. I slashed at her with a stick, but she dodged the blow and the stick broke in my hand. While I looked for another she reached a small pine, and climbed it like a cat. I threw a pebble at her, and she pitched headlong out of the top, apparently more in anger than in fright. Of course she came again to the ground with a thump. I charged again and she slipped around a stump. I got between her and the fence, and she peered at me over the top of stump with glaring eyes and open beak. All this time she kept up a constant stream of shrieks and yells which were most disconcerting. I grabbed at her head, looking out for the sharp claws, and swung her around to twist her neck. It was like leather, and all I succeeded in doing was to cut a deep gash in my hand on the edge of the ivory bill which is sharp as a knife. At this I dropped her, and she promptly hopped away into the fence, chattering louder than ever, and looking disheveled and fierce. I was now flustered and rather out of temper, so I banged at her with sticks or clods or anything I could lay my hands on. There were no stones. But in spite of me she reached the foot of a large tree which she began to climb with great rapidity. Conquered at last, I had resort to my gun, and used the other barrel rather savagely, I fear, and in disregard of feathers and science.

But she made a good specimen, nevertheless. If my readers happen to visit the Smithsonian Institution, the bird of this adventure will be found among the collection which formed part of the exhibit of the Institution at the Chicago Fair. She can be identified by the loss of about the eighth of an inch of her lower mandible, which was carried away by a shot at my second discharge.

A few minutes afterward I secured her mate as he came flying by to investigate, and flushed and bleeding but triumphant I bore my trophies into camp. During the week of our stay, we secured nearly a dozen specimens, most of which were sent in by Mr. Nelson to Dr. Merriam of the Department of Agriculture at Washington. Three skins that I made up under his direction were afterward secured for the Smithsonian. We found a further illustration of the toughness of this bird in the difficulty of removing the skin. It clings to the body in the most stubborn manner, and is so strong that it can scarcely be torn in the fingers.

Campephilus imperialis is about the size of a crow. Both sexes have a beautiful crest, the top of which curls forward. It and the back of the head in the male are bright red. In the female the head and crest are jet black. The principal color of the body is a glossy black, with beautiful markings of white on the back and wings. The beak is a rich yellow, closely resembling ivory, and is a marvel of strength and size. The range of this bird is not very well known, and it was not supposed to be so abundant anywhere as we found it among the pine-clad hills of Michoacan. So far as I know, its eggs are still unknown to science. It nests in high, dry pine trunks, where climbing for the eggs would be both difficult and dangerous.

Mr. Nelson on the same expedition discovered a new and very fine genus of pocket gophers. An account of the two species secured, as well as many other interesting things about the family, will be found in American Fauna, No. 8, a Bulletin issued by the Department of Agriculture at Washington.

G. B. Winton

Handwritten note at bottom:
Address;
Geo. B. Winton
San Antonio, Texas

_____

With an estimated 160 mounted specimens and study skins in museums around the world[6], very few scientists have experienced, studied, and published writings about the imperial woodpecker. The last verified documentation of a live bird was recently made available to science in a film of short duration from 1956 by an amateur ornithologist and is the only known photographic record of the imperial woodpecker[7]. Nelson had never seen a live imperial woodpecker prior to the sighting in Patzcuaro, but was clearly familiar with the species, most likely as a result of his studying specimens in the National Museum. To have detailed written record of these interactions and the behavior of this fascinating and relatively unknown bird has to be, in my opinion, invaluable to science today.

A thorough review of both Nelson and Goldman's field notebooks reveal that several imperial woodpecker specimens were secured during their 1892 trip on October 5th and 19th. Nelson's notes revealed that eight birds were taken; however, Goldman's field notes total only six specimens. Documentation also indicates that they saw the imperial woodpecker in other locations in Mexico during their explorations.

More widely known in Mexico as the *pitoreal*, the imperial woodpecker has not been scientifically verified in the wild since 1956 and is now thought to be extinct. Officially, it is listed as "Critically Endangered (Possibly Extinct)" by the International Union for Conservation of Nature (IUCN)[8]. A number of scientific expeditions have been undertaken over the years with the sole purpose of searching for living individuals, but all have failed. Active logging and habitat destruction, along with over-hunting (historically they've been used for food, medicinal purposes, and plumage for spiritual rituals), have accelerated population decline. Still today, local residents and workers in the Sierra Madre Occidental report sightings of this majestic bird. Ornithologists and researchers believe that unconfirmed sightings and the fact that multiple surveys have failed to find the species indicate that extinction is inevitable.

Is there hope? Many researchers and imperial woodpecker specialists believe that it is possible—however, highly unlikely—that a few surviving birds may live undetected in the mountainous regions of Mexico.

REFERENCES

[1] "Nelson and Goldman in Mexico." Available at http://cameratrapcodger.blogspot.com/2009/01/nelson-and-goldman-in-mexico. html. Retrieved on December 13, 2018.

[2] "Mexican Biodiversity." Available at http://vivanatura.org/mexican-biodiversity. Retrieved on December 13, 2018.

[3] "Only 12 vaquita porpoises remain, watchdog group reports." Available at www.news.mongabay.com. Retrieved on December 13, 2018.

[4] "'Extinct' tiny shrew rediscovered." Available at http://news.bbc.co.uk/earth/hi/earth_news/newsid_8152000/8152862.stm. Re-trieved on December 13, 2018.

[5] Xavier Lopez-Medellin and Rodrigo A. Medellin. "The Influence of E. W. Nelson and E. A. Goldman on Mexican Mammalogy." p.93, January, 2016.

[6] "Imperial Woodpecker." Available at https://en.wikipedia.org/wiki/Imperial_woodpecker. Retrieved on December 13, 2018.

[7] Martjan Lammertink, Tim W. Gallagher, Kenneth V. Rosenberg, et al. "Film Documentation of the Probably Extinct Imperial Woodpecker (Campephilus imperialis)." The Auk, 128(4): 671-677· October, 2011.

[8] "Campephilus imperialis." IUCN Red List of Threatened Species. Version 2018.2. International Union for Conservation of Nature. Retrieved on December 13, 2018.

www.ingramcontent.com/pod-product-compliance
Lightning Source LLC
Chambersburg PA
CBHW040025050426
42452CB00003B/143